In *Take My Hand and Walk with Me*, Pam Goss invites us to take God's hand and walk with Him in the dark days. In her warm, engaging style, she digs deep inside to share from her personal experiences of both joy and pain. In her journey, she discovers closer intimacy with God.

I learned more about the truth of God's *right hand* as Pam wove Scripture into every page. My quiet time filled with the unsearchable and transformational riches that God's Word offers.

As I read, I felt myself drawn to Pam, desiring to hold her hand and those of others, as we were never meant to walk alone. *Take My Hand* has inspired me to walk close to God and with one another. I highly recommend this inspiring devotional.

—Ruth Coghill, author,
The *WOW* series Bibles studies and
*Unborn. Untold. True Stories of Abortion
and God's healing Grace*

D1300618

Learn to Trust

God's Guidance

on the

Darkest of Days

TAKE my HAND and WALK WITH ME

Pamela Goss

TAKE MY HAND AND WALK WITH ME
Copyright © 2020 by Pamela Goss

Pictures are by the author except the cover photo by Denisse Espadas, Chapter 7 by Margaret Dorman, Chapter 8 by Stephanie Goss, Chapters 12 and 13 by Hilary Tyne, Chapter 14 by Marcia Goss, and Chapter 16 by Jorge Pinto, used by permission.

Printed in Canada

ISBN: 978-1-4866-1876-7
eBook ISBN: 978-1-4866-1877-4

Word Alive Press
119 De Baets Street Winnipeg, MB R2J 3R9
www.wordalivepress.ca

Cataloguing in Publication information can be obtained from Library and Archives Canada.

For my precious jewels,
Sophia, Reuben, Joey,
Zach, Robin, and Leo
who fill my life with love and laughter.

CONTENTS

INTRODUCTION

When the path we are on becomes rocky and hard to navigate, and it takes everything you have to keep persevering, this is the time to take hold of the right hand of the Almighty God. From his hand, freely offered to you, will flow wisdom and mercy and power. His hand brought the world into being, and in his hand is the life of every creature and the breath of all mankind. (Job 12:9-10) Take his all-powerful hand and he will go through your trials with you, in all ways and at all times, because he loves you unconditionally and will never let you go. He wants to bring you through to a place of abundance, so never give up. As you go through this book, you will discover wonderful ways that God blesses you when you take his right hand in yours.

Their road is dark and rough
but I will give light to keep them from stumbling.
This is my solemn promise.
(Isaiah 42:16, CEV)

CHAPTER ONE

A New Creation

*Sing to the Lord a new song, for he has done
marvelous things; his right hand and his holy
arm have worked salvation for him.*
(Psalm 98:1, NIV)

*The promise: God says to take his hand and
walk with him, and he will give us a new song
to sing and make us a new creation.*

How joyful it is when we first start out on this new life. We feel light and free as our sins are forgiven and he creates in us a pure heart and a steadfast spirit (Psalm 51:10, NIV). God has a good plan for us. All through the years of our life, he has been preparing us to fulfill our calling, giving us a passion for life. Our days are filled with deep satisfaction as we follow him. His will is the path to a fulfilled life, even though it can be rocky and hard. He supplies just the right equipment for our journey, so that we find ourselves doing far more than we ever dreamed. This life of purpose becomes one of abundant fruit and lasting satisfaction. It is worth any sacrifice we have to make to follow his leading.

"And God is able to make all grace abound to you, so that in all things, at all times, having all that you need, you will abound in every good work" (2 Corinthians 9:8, BSB). In this context, 'able' comes from the Greek word *dunamis* meaning abundant strength, miraculous power, or mighty works. It's where we get the word *dynamite*. This mighty, explosive power is available to us exactly when we need it in perfect supply out of his abundance. How awesome is that? Nothing shall be impossible for us, for it is his strength that enables us to be overcomers.

The takeaway: If we walk with him,
we will be empowered.

For we are God's workmanship, created in Christ Jesus to do good works, which God prepared in advance as our way of life. (Ephesians 2:10, BSB)

CHAPTER TWO

Never Alone

*So do not fear, for I am with you; do not be
dismayed, for I am your God. I will strengthen
you and help you; I will uphold you
with my righteous right hand.*
(Isaiah 41:10, NIV)

*The promise: God promises that if we take his
hand and walk with him, we will never be
alone again.*

God, knowing that sin separates us from himself, sent his son Jesus to pay the price of our sins by dying on the cross. Jesus loves us so much that, even if you were the only one to have sinned, he would still have died for you. Our part is trusting in his finished work, confessing our sins, and turning from the path we are on to commit our lives to him. We will never be the same, having been changed and filled with his Holy Spirit who will guide and help us on our journey. It is a choice you will never regret.

We are engraved on the palms of his hands (Isaiah 49:16) and he will never forget us. What a picture of how much we are cherished by him! Nothing can ever separate us from his love, *"… neither death nor life, neither angels nor demons, neither the present nor the future, nor any powers, neither height nor depth, nor anything else in all creation…"* (Romans 8:38-39, NIV).

He knows us by name and longs to have fellowship with us. Give it all to him, for he cares for us as an eagle cares for its own. *"He was like an eagle building its nest that flutters over its young. It spreads its wings to catch them and carries them on its feathers"* (Deuteronomy 32:11, NCV). This is God smiling down on us, lovingly caring for our every need and lifting us up to soar to new heights. How glorious!

Right away, he starts transforming us into his likeness and fulfilling his plans for us. We can know that anything that comes into our lives is for a purpose and is filtered through his fingers of love.

In 1950's Ontario there was a polio epidemic. In 1955, at the age of three months, I contracted the disease. It left me with severe muscle loss, mostly in my legs and feet. With corrective surgeries, I led a very normal life. Then, when I was 33, that polio came back with a vengeance, leaving me much weaker and with chronic pain. How I prayed, along with many others, for relief and healing. God had a different plan for me though, so I have learned to be in daily prayer for his sustaining grace (divine favour) and for strength to handle whatever each day brings.

Simply talking to him throughout the day has led to a greater intimacy with my Saviour. As he has proven himself to me over and over, I now trust him totally. He is always with me and is my constant companion. So our prayers were answered in many better ways than instant healing. This life is slippery and it can easily careen out of control, like stepping on a patch of ice, but with God holding our hand, we have a strong arm to guide us.

> *The takeaway: If we walk with him,*
> *he will keep our feet from slipping.*

But those who hope in the Lord will renew their strength. They will soar on wings like eagles; they will run and not grow weary, they will walk and not be faint. (Isaiah 40:31, NIV)

CHAPTER THREE
Satisfaction

*You protect me with your saving shield. You
support me with your right hand. You have
stooped to make me great (significant).*
(Psalm 18:35, NCV)

*The promise: If we take God's hand and walk
with him, he will satisfy the longings
of our soul.*

For fulfillment in life, we look to many things such as a career,
making money, family, friends, and fame. Often, our great
desire is to find that special someone who will love and cherish us.

These are all good things, but they will never fully satisfy
because each of us has a God-shaped vacuum that only Jesus

can fill. He satisfies our innermost places, all of our hungers and longings.

The psalmist says, *"Taste and see that the Lord is good!"* (Psalm 34:8a, NIV) He is the bread that gives us all the nourishment we could ever need for life. *"... Whoever feeds on this bread will live forever"* (John 6:58b, NIV). He causes us to shine like stars in the darkness (Philippians 2:15) for he is the light of the world.

One of those stars was Bill Graham, who died in 2019 after a long battle with cancer. His wife Lorraine lovingly cared for him at home, and friends and family visited often. He was cheerful and took an interest in the concerns of others, even though he was suffering. Bill had a wonderful presence of peace, for he knew he was going to Heaven to be with Jesus. *"For we know that if the earthly tent we live in is destroyed, we have a building from God, an eternal house in heaven, not built by human hands"* (2 Corinthians 5:1, NIV). Cancer had no power to take eternal life from Bill. One of my favourite memories was Bill calling and saying, "It's Billy Graham" and then laughing infectiously. We miss him, but we know we will meet again in Heaven.

We are refreshed by the wind of the Holy Spirit given to indwell us as our comforter, counselor, helper, and guide. The pure oil of the Holy Spirit fuels our lamps, continually giving off a beautiful and unique fragrance—the fragrance of Christ.

When we believe, our risen Saviour gives us his Holy Spirit as "living water", which satisfies our thirst, bubbling up like a spring to eternal life (John 7:38-39). As this living water flows in and through us, we are renewed.

This is God smiling down on us, meeting our every hunger and longing. No one can love you like he does, held in his loving arms with an unfailing love that will never die. He will never leave you or forsake you, but will lovingly care for you.

The takeaway: If we take God's hand,
we will be totally satisfied.

You open your hand and satisfy the desires of every living thing. (Psalm 145:16, NIV)

CHAPTER FOUR

Watched Over

*If I rise on the wings of the dawn, if I settle on
the far side of the sea, even there your hand will
guide me, your right hand will hold me fast.*
(Psalm 139:9-10, NIV)

*The promise: If we take God's hand, he will
never let us go.*

Our lives can change in an instant, and we wonder how we can ever survive this heartbreaking trial. We don't have to go through this alone—God is right there, our storm shelter and our refuge. He collects our tears in his bottle, and he keeps a record of our sufferings (Psalm 56:8).

My life changed dramatically at age 7, when my dad died from a heart attack and my mom had to go to work full time. Many times I faced heartaches and loneliness. God's gift to me, during these years, was my sister-in-law Betty Hayes, who allowed me to be such a big part of their lives. She was a wonderful example of how to be a great mom, and I had the joy of loving up my niece and nephews. All these experiences were great preparation for fostering hurting children.

It is in times like these that we can rest on God's promises and see him at work more than any other. The test becomes our testimony. He goes with us every step of the way, and we see his faithfulness in never leaving us or forsaking us. I also have the blessing of members of my church family who are always there, offering encouragement and covering me in prayer. God also sends wonderful friends to help us along our journey when we need them. He is a giver of good gifts and loves to give even more extravagantly than we ask.

> I asked God for water, He gave me an ocean.
> I asked God for a flower, He gave me a garden.
> I asked God for a tree, He gave me a forest.
> I asked God for a friend, He gave me you. (Unknown)

How I cherish each of my friends who have shown me what it means to be a Christian and covered me with prayer like a sweet, fragrant incense rising up to God. Jesus himself, at God's right hand, also intercedes for us (Romans 8:34). He will open the eyes of our hearts to see the deeper things of God, and we will grow so close to him, so intimate. We might not always know the why, but we can trust that he knows and has a purpose in allowing our trials. Trust in his unconditional love. There are no accidents for the child of God. Even when we go through a fiery ordeal, we have hope that we will see *"the goodness of the Lord in the land of the living"* (Psalm 27:13b, NIV). He will bring us through in his perfect will and time. We cannot go anywhere where we won't be held in the loving, powerful hand of God. He doesn't let go but holds us fast.

God, as our loving heavenly Father, knows all about us. We have an intimate relationship, and he lovingly keeps us in his sights always. As we are the apple of his eye, he delights to bless us and watch over us with our best interests at heart. We are so very precious to him.

> *The takeaway: If we walk with him,*
> *he will bring us through.*

And we know that in all things God works for the good of those who love him, who have been called according to his purpose. (Romans 8:28, NIV)

CHAPTER FIVE

Forgiveness

*Show me the wonders of your great love, you
who save by your right hand...*
(Psalm 17:7a, NIV)

*The promise: If we take God's hand and walk
with him, we will know real peace.*

God is so full of unfailing love for you that he desires to
have a relationship with you and give you the love you are
looking for.

God sent his only Son to die on the cross for you so that
your sins can be washed away. As you confess and receive
forgiveness, he will cast your sins in the sea of forgetfulness and

will never remember them again. Be real with God, and forgive yourself and others. *"... If someone does wrong to you, forgive that person because the Lord forgave you"* (Colossians 3:13b, NCV).

Unforgiveness is as harmful to you as drinking poison, for it will slowly eat away at you, stealing your peace and joy. God will repay those who hurt you—he is your vindicator. *"Do not take revenge, my dear friends, but leave room for God's wrath, for it is written: 'It is mine to avenge; I will repay,' says the Lord"* (Romans 12:19, NIV).

One day all will be revealed. Trust him with your heartache, and he will turn that spirit of bitterness and anger into one of love. The peace of God that passes human understanding will fill your spirit, for Jesus came to set us free. On that day, God will clothe us with his robe of righteousness (Isaiah 61:10), which is purity of character, and our souls will rejoice. Our hearts will be filled with thankfulness for his great love and faithfulness.

The takeaway: If we walk with him,
we will live a free and full life.

Be kind and compassionate to one another, forgiving each other, just as in Christ God forgave you." (Ephesians 4:32, NIV)

CHAPTER SIX

No Fear

*For I am the Lord your God who takes hold of
your right hand and says to you, Do not fear; I
will help you.*
(Isaiah 41:13, NIV)

*The promise: If we take God's hand and walk
with him, we will never be controlled by fear.*

Fear can imprison us. Our lives can be so filled with fear that
we are stymied from really living. We can fear losing our
jobs, our health, our loved ones, our finances—in other words,
our future. Fear can actually make us physically ill.

That's when it is time to claim the promises of God. He is there for us in all ways, and he wants to help us be free from fear. We are so loved by him. Psalm 103:8 (NIV) says, *"The Lord is compassionate and gracious, slow to anger, abounding in love."* We can trust him fully, in all areas of our lives, knowing he is faithful and will take care of us. *"Cast all your anxiety on him because he cares for you"* (1 Peter 5:7, NIV).

When I start to be afraid, I say Psalm 23 to myself, and I am comforted. As our shepherd, he lovingly meets our needs out of his compassionate heart. As he is our father, we can run into his arms and lean on him. *"For we have heard of your faith in Christ Jesus [the leaning of your entire human personality on Him in absolute trust and confidence in His power, wisdom, and goodness]…"* (Colossians 1:4a, AMPC). He replaces all our fears with peace, since we know that he is all-powerful.

Praise God, he did this for me when I committed my life to him shortly after I was married in 1975. Before that, I was very fearful and it often held me back. Now when I do come to a scary situation, I continue in faith, knowing he will help me every step of the way. God is good and he wants to bless us, but sometimes that means stepping out of our comfort zone. When we do, God goes with us so we can be strong and courageous and not give up (Deuteronomy 31:6).

As we keep our eyes fixed on him, we are never shaken, for he is our rock on which we firmly stand. Think of what it's like to be standing on a high, majestic mountain. The greatest, most awe-inspiring experience of all is standing on the rock who is Jesus.

The takeaway: If we walk with him,
we know he has us in his grip.

I sought the Lord, and he answered me; he delivered me
from all my fears. (Psalm 34:4, NIV)

CHAPTER SEVEN

A New Heart

Save us and help us with your right hand, that
those you love may be delivered.
(Psalm 60:5, NIV)

The promise: If we take his hand and walk with
him, we will have a brand new life.

When we place our lives in Jesus' hands, we receive a spiritual heart transplant. Our hearts are filled with his Holy Spirit, and we are made new. *"I will give you a new heart and put a new spirit in you: I will remove from you your heart of stone and give you a heart of flesh. And I will put my Spirit in you..."* (Ezekiel 36:26-27a, NIV).

We gain peace with God when we submit to him. His Word becomes precious to us as we cherish his truths in our hearts. As we lift our faces to God, we find delight and he hears our prayers (Job 22:26-27).

Jesus is our vine and we are the branches, so we need pruning if we are going to bear fruit. God, our good gardener, uses circumstances to cut away diseased bits. Then we can start to produce the fruit of the spirit—love, joy, peace, long-suffering, kindness, goodness, faithfulness, gentleness, and self-control. In the same way that vines are lifted up to receive more air and sun, so God does to us just what we need. Then, like a tree planted by the water, we produce abundant fruit.

As we use these fruits to bless others, God is glorified. Day by day, we are being transformed into the Lord's likeness and we are his reflection to others (2 Corinthians 3:18).

The takeaway: If we take his hand,
we will be transformed.

Do not conform to the pattern of this world, but be transformed by the renewing of your mind. Then you will be able to test and approve what God's will is—his good, pleasing and perfect will. (Romans 12:2, NIV)

CHAPTER EIGHT

Friend

Yet I am always with you;
you hold me by my right hand.
(Psalm 73:23, NIV)

The promise: We take God's hand and walk
with him because he loves us.

Proverbs 17:17 tells us that a friend loves at all times, and this is true of Jesus. He longs to come alongside you and share in your journey. He wants to listen and to give you wisdom for the path you are on. You can tell him all your hopes and dreams, and then you may find that it is God who has put those hopes and dreams within you to fulfill his wonderful plan for your life. Our lives have a greater purpose that God wants us to fulfill. He is the *"friend who sticks closer than a brother"* (Proverbs 18:24b, NIV) and wants to lead, guide, and help you to bring those dreams to life.

All my life, I loved babies and my desire was to be a mom. Those desires gave me a heart for hurting children and led me to become a foster mom for thirty-five years. Wholeheartedly, I followed this path, and how I loved helping children turn their lives around. This was so challenging and humbling as, many times, not knowing what to do, I sought the Lord's wisdom and guidance.

God also sends us wonderful friends to support us and encourage us—friends to laugh and cry with us on our journey. I can always count on their prayers and loyalty. Sometimes they needed to show tough love in order to get me back on the right track. It is a true friend who loves you enough to speak up. *"Wounds from a friend can be trusted…"* (Proverbs 27:6a, NIV).

God know us so intimately that he knows the number of hairs on our heads (Matthew 10:30), proof that he is someone who is constantly caring for us, seeing our needs, and longing for our companionship.

The takeaway: If we take his hand,
he will never leave our side.

"… to grasp how wide and long and high and deep is the love of Christ, and to know this love that surpasses knowledge…" (Ephesians 3:18b, 19a, NIV)

CHAPTER NINE

Joy

You will show me the path of life; in Your presence is fullness of joy; In Your right hand there are pleasures forevermore.
(Psalm 16:11, AMP)

The promise: God says that if we take his hand, we will know fullness of joy.

This path of life we are on holds both blessings and sorrows, but we can know joy, an "exuberance for life" (MSG), even on our darkest days. Happiness comes and goes, but joy can be permanent. Joy is confidence that God is in control and trust that he is working all things out for our good in his way and time. This joy of the Lord is our strength (Nehemiah 8:10). Joy goes hand in hand with our faith and hope, and this is what enables us to live in victory.

When trouble looms over us like a mountain of sorrow and hopelessness, if we take his hand, Christ will infuse us with his inner strength, enabling us to handle whatever comes. *"Though they stumble, they will never fall, for the Lord holds them by the hand"* (Psalm 37:24, NLT). How safe and secure we feel knowing God has us in his care. Blessed and happy are those who walk in the light of the Lord's presence (Psalm 89:15).

Immerse yourself in God's Word, for *"God's Word is a life map for us, showing the way to joy"* (Psalm 19:8, MSG). As we study it, we grow in our confidence that God is faithful and that, ultimately, good will come.

Spend time with God outdoors, and you will be lifted up. It becomes easier to believe in his ability to help us as we witness his imaginative and glorious handiwork everywhere we look. Joy comes as we keep our minds focused on who Jesus is, our Ebenezer, or stone of help. This rock on which we stand is all-powerful, and so our hopeless-looking situation doesn't seem so impossible.

Think about how God has been there for you in the past, and know that he will be now, loving and caring for you. *"We wait in hope for the Lord; he is our help and our shield"* (Psalm 33:20, NIV). Great joy flows within us as we grow closer to our Savior and trust in his vast, unfailing love which surrounds us (Psalm 32:10).

One of my mountains to climb was the time my haemoglobin kept dropping, leaving me close to death. The doctors were stymied. I was unable to function, and my mom came and took care of my young family. My doctor gave me his home phone number and said to call him anytime, so I knew my situation was very serious. With my heart breaking, I wrote a letter to each of my four children in case I wasn't alive when they grew up. God was with me through those many months. Then, praise him, he lifted me up to health once again as my haemoglobin slowly climbed back up to normal.

Now I know, without a doubt, that my life is in his hands. All those mundane tasks of running a household have become something I am so thankful to do. *"I'll convert their weeping into laughter, lavishing comfort, invading their grief with joy"* (Jeremiah 31:13, MSG). How thankful I am now to have the joy of loving my grandchildren.

Praise God for he is awesome, majestic, and holy—powerful enough to move your mountain. He will turn your valley of sorrow into a spring full of blessings. As his hand of mercy moves in your life, delivering you, your testimony will be, *"... the Lord's right hand has done mighty things!"* (Psalm 118:16b, NIV)

> *The takeaway: If we take his hand,*
> *we will be delivered.*

Save us and help us with your right hand, that those you love may be delivered. (Psalm 108:6, NIV)

CHAPTER TEN

Helper

*Though I walk in the midst of trouble, you
preserve my life. You stretch out your hand
against the anger of my foes; with your right
hand you save me."*
(Psalm 138:7, NIV)

*The promise: If we take God's hand and walk
with him, he will give us wisdom
to lead a balanced life.*

God is the one who is there to help in all of life's battles. Sometimes, though, we become physically exhausted from doing too much, and God knows we need rest, even just a good night's sleep. Maybe it's a bigger rest that we need, as in the twenty-third Psalm where he makes us lie down in green pastures.

One of those times occurred when my doctor informed me that I was a step away from a total breakdown. He started me on medication and gave me a prescription for a week of rest and relaxation. He said, "Go and see your daughter out west." I thought this was an impossible feat, as I didn't have the money for a plane ticket. Then my friend, Hilary Tyne, generously gave me the money, and my husband lovingly said he would take care of the kids. Being with my daughter Marcia in the majestic mountains of Alberta restored my soul.

Is your battle emotional? Hurtful situations with a friend, family, or church family member can leave us feeling very raw. Still, difficult people can teach us important lessons. God can give us a new perspective and a new heart of love for them. He can help us to forgive and have the wisdom to know how to handle whatever is happening.

A spiritual battle—when we feel God is far away—can be the most difficult of all. Those feelings can be fickle and deceptive, for he is always there, waiting to step in and renew us again. *"Come near to God and he will come near to you..."* (James 4:8a, NIV) So get into his Word and claim his promises. You will find your faith renewed as you see your prayers answered. You can have absolute trust in him, for he is always good and his heart is full of mercy and compassion towards us. *"So we say with confidence, 'The Lord is my helper; I will not be afraid...'"* (Hebrews 13:6a, NIV).

In all our troubles, he will help us through, providing whatever we need at the right time. Sometimes, we can't see the big picture—like the back of a tapestry, all we can see is a mess of tangled threads and colours. But God is taking that mess and making something beautiful out of it all. Someday, we will see the picture from the front and realize that God created a masterpiece.

The takeaway: If we take his hand,
we will be restored.

Restore us, God Almighty; make your face shine upon us, that we may be saved. (Psalm 80:7, NIV)

CHAPTER ELEVEN

Victory

*It was not by their sword that they won the
land, nor did their arm bring them victory; it
was your right hand, your arm, and the light of
your face, for you loved them.*
(Psalm 44:3, NIV)

*The promise: If we take God's hand and walk
with him, we will be victorious.*

When we start out on this journey with the Lord and get
into his Word, the Bible, we see that a lot of changes
are needed in us. This can be overwhelming, and we can feel
downcast, but we need to take our Christian growth one day

at a time. The good news is that it is God who changes us from the inside out. As we start to grow spiritually, becoming more Christ-like, this will begin to show in the way we live in all areas of our lives.

We find ourselves putting others first, being more compassionate and merciful, even caring about the unlovely. We seek to have the same servant attitude of Jesus, who washed his disciples' feet even though that was considered a very lowly thing to do.

We become more forgiving, giving others the benefit of the doubt. Giving is something that we love to do, and we look for ways to bless others. We freely give, out of love, and it's exciting to see how God still meets all of our needs, sometimes in amazing ways. *"'... Test me in this,' says the Lord Almighty, 'and see if I will not throw open the flood gates of heaven and pour out so much blessing that there will not be enough room to store it'"* (Malachi 3:10, NIV). We cannot outgive God. *"Good will come to those who are generous and lend freely..."* (Psalm 112:5a, NIV)

We will become people of integrity who desire to be honest and trustworthy. Of course, there will be times when we mess up, but God's mercies are new every morning. A new day to start over, a gift of life from him whose love and faithfulness will never fail. Forgiveness is freely given so that we can be easily forgiving of others. God sees our hearts and his compassions never fail.

"But you are a chosen people, a royal priesthood, a holy nation, God's special possession, that you may declare the praises of him who called you out of darkness into his wonderful light" (1 Peter 2:9,

NIV). We are his beloved, his children, and we live to bring glory to God with our lives. As he is transforming us through the power of the Holy Spirit who lives in us, we become the righteousness of God. This is victorious living!

*The takeaway: If we walk with him,
he will sanctify us.*

The Lord is good to those whose hope is in him, to the one who seeks him... (Lamentations 3:25, NIV)

CHAPTER TWELVE

Polished

Your right hand, Lord, was majestic in power.
Your right hand, Lord, shattered the enemy.
(Exodus 15:6, NIV)

The promise: If we take God's hand and walk
with him, we will be powerful.

The Lord is a warrior (Exodus 15:3). Just as a warrior keeps his quiver within easy reach and guards it closely, so too does the Lord keep us. We are his arrows to be used for his purposes. He keeps us close while he is polishing us by sending certain experiences and trials to prepare us for what he is calling us to do. As we go through these times, our jagged, dark bits are being ground off. These dark bits are things like complaining, lying, gossiping, being deceitful, and treating others badly—all our un-Christ-like behaviours. He wants us to always act in love, helping to meet the needs of others and live unselfishly. All this polishing will make us shine like stars. Then, when we are ready, he sends us out swiftly and surely, like an arrow, bringing all the glory to him with what we accomplish. So keep your eyes open. It is possible that an annoying interruption is really a God appointment.

The takeaway: If we walk with him,
he will send us soaring.

"... in the shadow of his hand he hid me; he made me into a polished arrow and concealed me in his quiver." (Isaiah 49:2b, NIV)

CHAPTER THIRTEEN

Security

*I have set the Lord always before me; because he
is at my right hand, I shall not be shaken.*
(Psalm 16:8, ESV)

*The promise: If we take God's hand and walk
with him, we will live worry-free.*

We have many pressures and trials in our lives. God never promised a problem-free life, but he has promised to be with us through everything. There is a wonderful rest in that, knowing we are securely in God's hands. All around us the storm is raging, but inside we are calm. We are not shaken, for he is our rock, our fortress and refuge.

One very challenging time in my life really proved the truth of this. In 2006, we had three very needy foster children. That year, my elderly mom, who needed lots of care, came to live with us too. I must have been praying for patience, LOL. God provided help in so many ways. Good friends supported me and were excellent listeners. My brothers gave financially so that I could hire help, and God sent a wonderful woman who helped with house cleaning and truly cared for my mom. They developed a good friendship. My brother Mike was especially helpful as he was always someone I could count on for support. Of course, there were many frustrations, but I learned the truth of *"I can do all this through him who gives me strength"* (Philippians 4:13, NIV). Then came the heartache of placing my mom in a nursing home as her health needs escalated and brought new challenges of care. My spunky mom embraced the changes and she made new friends, but there were many tearful times too, and my heart broke for her. She almost made her goal of living to a hundred, but died at the age of ninety-nine. I miss her every day.

There is a wonderful painting by Jack E. Dawson called, "Peace in the Midst of the Storm". It shows a bird sitting on her nest in the cleft of a rock with her baby chicks tucked under her and a fierce storm raging around them. David implored God to, "... hide me in the shadow of your wings" (Psalm 17:8b, NIV). There is no safer place, and because we have such a feeling of security, we lift up our voices and sing (Psalm 63:7).

The takeaway: If we take God's hand,
he will cover us with his wings.

He alone is my rock and my salvation. He is my fortress; I
will never be shaken. (Psalm 62:2, BSV)

CHAPTER FOURTEEN

Hope

… for the Lord upholds him with his hand.
(Psalm 37:24b, NIV)

*The promise: If we take God's hand and walk
with him, he will uphold us.*

When we place our hand in his and are upheld by his hand, we experience so many blessings. We see his power and his glory as he works in our lives; we experience His love for us and the deep satisfaction of living for Him. Then, no matter what, we have a deep abiding joy. Our hearts overflow with praise and thankfulness for who God is and his faithfulness in daily bearing our burdens and giving us strength (Psalm 68:19).

Sometimes, our father's heart of love simply wants to bless us because he loves us so. One summer, many of our children and grandchildren were coming for two weeks to stay at the cottage—something that the Lord has blessed us with as well, and which we felt was perfect for our family. I knew, with our shoreline, that it wouldn't be easy for the little ones. A couple of days before they came, a huge, inflatable raft floated to our dock. We tied it up and let the police know, in case the owner was looking for it. That raft provided lots of fun for everyone, especially for the younger ones.

A couple of days after our family left, the owner called to claim it. We were amazed when we learned how far it had travelled across the water. Joy filled my heart as I realized that the Lord had indeed provided the perfect solution and with perfect timing. As our heavenly Father, he delights in giving us good gifts.

When we get to know who God is, it becomes easy to trust him with our lives. He is a strong tower, our stronghold in the day of trouble (Nahum 1:7, NKJV). The Lord is good. He is our sun, lighting the way, and the Alpha and Omega who goes before and behind us. He is our strength when we have a battle to fight. God says, "Do not be afraid; do not be discouraged. Go out to face them tomorrow, and the Lord will be with you" (2 Chronicles 20:17b, NIV). He is our shield, always on the alert, ever watchful over us (1 Peter 3:12).

Our all powerful God is on our side to help us achieve the victory. As the battle rages, we can stand firm, even singing and praising God, because we have hope, knowing we are held in his hands of love and mercy. "The Lord your God wins victory after victory and is always with you. He celebrates and sings because of you, and he will refresh your life with his love" (Zephaniah 3:17, CEV).

God never changes. He is the "I AM", referring to his abiding, eternal, steadfast, and dependable nature. "I AM" says that he is the Almighty, the eternally constant God. He knows us and sees us. We are precious to him and he loves us (Isaiah 43:4).

> *The takeaway: If we walk with him,*
> *we will experience a deep, abiding love.*

... have faith in the Lord your God and you will be upheld.
(2 Chronicles 20:20b, NIV)

CHAPTER FIFTEEN

Confidence

Now I know that the Lord saves his anointed;
He will answer him from His holy heaven with
the saving strength of his right hand.
(Psalm 20:6, AMP)

The promise: If we take God's hand and walk
with him, we can have confidence
that he will help us.

God has a good plan for our lives and knows the future. Jeremiah 29:11 says that his plans are to prosper us and not to harm us, to give us hope and a future.

Sometimes, we are faced with deep troubles such as exhausting chronic pain, a diagnosis like the scary "big C", the shattering heartbreak of a spouse wanting out of the marriage, debilitating depression, bleak financial troubles, or the devastating loss of a loved one. Whatever your trial is, it can turn your world upside down, and it can be awhile before you can get your feet on solid ground again. This can feel very unfair to us and even scary as we look ahead.

God tells us not to fear, for we do not walk alone. He will go through this with us, hand in hand, strengthening us. Nothing is ever in vain. Even when someone sets out to harm us, he can bring good from it. For this, we have Jesus. Lay everything before God, give it all to him, and he will handle it in his way and time. He will see us through to the other side and make a way where it all seems impossible. God will show himself to be your rock and your deliverer, and he can bring about good results against all odds. He is "… wonderfully holy, amazingly powerful, a worker of miracles" (Exodus 15:11b, NCV).

Isaiah 45:3 (ESV) says, "I will give you the treasures of darkness..." It's in those dark times that precious treasures are revealed. If we faithfully continue on, we will see that the most intricate and well-crafted work of all was done in those dark days. Treasures of goodness and beauty will come from your sufferings. The brightest diamonds grow in the darkest cavities of the earth.

As a result of having had polio, my left foot started going sideways and my toes were curling under, so my very clever surgeon, Dr. Veri, came up with a plan for foot reconstruction. I am so thankful for Dr. Veri, whose skills have kept me walking. After I had the surgery, I didn't walk for six months, and it was a long difficult battle to start walking again. During those months, God revealed himself to me, showing me treasures in my darkness. I wouldn't trade that time for anything, because in it I discovered more of the living Christ, an intimacy with my Saviour, and joy in my soul. This lead to my writing, "Songs in the Night."

As you trust God with your darkest nights, he will give you his peace, because you will know it is all part of his plan for you. Keep on walking by faith, even on your darkest paths, "... one foot at a time, down the path of peace" (Luke 1:79b, MSG). There is always hope, so don't give up!

The takeaway: If we walk with him,
he will be our light in the darkness.

The Lord their God will save his people on that day as a shepherd saves his flock. They will sparkle in his land like jewels in a crown. (Zechariah 9:16, NIV)

CHAPTER SIXTEEN

His Royal Bride

... at your right hand is the royal bride
in gold of Ophir.
(Psalm 45:9b, NIV)

The promise: If we walk with Jesus and take his
hand, we will be his bride.

Oh, how Jesus loves us and wants us to spend eternity with him. He invites us to come and be his, because we are so beautiful to him.

We see this picture of a royal wedding in Psalm 45, and it is a foreshadowing of the union between Christ and the church. To Jesus, we are the royal bride, his chosen one, his delight. He woos us with a love that is never-ending. This love is an agape love—Jesus sacrificed his well-being for our benefit when he died for us, and now he is our advocate. He calls us Hephzibah, which means *my delight is in her*. This abundant love, which makes us so precious in his sight, so cherished and treasured, binds our hearts to him.

At the wedding, there we will be rejoicing with exuberance, ecstatic joy, and delight. How glorious it will be! As our bridegroom, he is the perfect husband who will care for us and rejoice over us always (Isaiah 62:5). The bride will be given fine linen, radiant and clean, to wear, "… for the fine linen signifies the righteousness [the ethical conduct, personal integrity, moral courage, and godly character of believers] (Revelation 19:8, AMP).

What is his becomes ours as his bride. We are heirs of God and joint-heirs with Christ (Romans 8:17). We will be united for eternity, faithful to each other, and ever loyal. I am his and he is mine. "Though you have not seen him, you love him; and even though you do not see him now, you believe in him and are filled with an inexpressible and glorious joy" (1 Peter 1:8, NIV). His desires become our desires, for we are so passionately loved.

The takeaway: If we take his hand,
we will be surrounded by beauty, joy, and love.

Let us rejoice and be glad and give him glory! For the wedding of the Lamb has come, and his bride has made herself ready. (Revelation 19:7, NIV)

Sheltered In Place
A Poem by Heather Fraser Kirby

Hold me in your tender hands, Lord Jesus.
Shelter me in hands scarred so deeply,
by the fierce weight hung on you, on that tree.
Not the mere weight of your body,
which alone would have done sufficient damage,
but the vast weight of my self-reliant heart.
Our private and corporate willful independence.
Our outright refusal to acknowledge your sacrifice, for each of us.

Hands that mere days before had held a child, refreshed the deaf,
sighted the blind, healed a harlot's heart, raised the dead to life.
Each of them an element of my need to be held, restored,
resuscitated.
My need: to be sheltered in the holy hollow of Jehovah Jireh.
Sustaining hands. Eternal hands that continue to bear us,
your children, bought by your blood, before your Father's throne.

Let me hear the whisper of your words, Lord:
'Come weary one, take my hand.
The plans I have for you are full of hope, promise, truth.
Seek me out in life's marketplace or in your solitude.
Call on me.
Exchange the weight of your discouragement,
for my gentle discipling and grace.
Be nourished. Be refreshed.

Journey with me.
I promise you
my rest, my peace, my joy.
Come, Child, come to Me!' [1]

Sheltered in Place used with permission of the author, Heather Fraser Kirby.

---

[1] Kirby, Heather Fraser " Sheltered in Place" (unpublished poem, 2008), typescript.

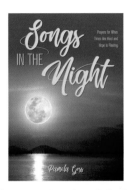

Songs In the Night

Your life can change in the blink of any eye. Unexpectedly, something happens that turns your world upside-down. You're blindsided and overwhelmed. It seems like you have a mountain to climb every day.

This book of prayers will help you through such a time, offering hope and encouragement. God is waiting to hear from you, to come alongside and give you strength. He cares about you and loves you deeply. Even in your darkest circumstances, there can be hope and even joy!

AUTHOR BIO:

Pamela Goss is a wife, mom, and gigi (grandma), as well as a foster mom for thirty-five years. She lives with her husband John and a sweet cocker spaniel named Lucy in beautiful Bobcaygeon. She loves times with her family, cottage life, and playing Scrabble online with people around the globe.

Contact Pamela at pamela31songs@gmail.com.

Check out her Facebook page for encouraging words
at Pamela Goss – Author